MALINI

MALINI

By

Rabindranath Tagore

Translated into English by the Author

Introduction

Nirmal Kanti Bhattacharjee

NIYOGI
BOOKS

Published by

NIYOGI BOOKS

D-78, Okhla Industrial Area, Phase-I
New Delhi-110 020, INDIA
Tel: 91-11-26816301, 49327000
Fax: 91-11-26810483, 26813830
email: niyogibooks@gmail.com
website: www.niyogibooks.com

ISBN: 978-93-81523-19-3

Publication: 2012

All rights are reserved. No part of this publication may be reproduced or
transmitted in any form or by any means, electronic or mechanical, including
photocopying, recording or by any information storage and retrieval system
without prior written permission and consent of the Publisher.

Cover Design: Global Publishing Solutions, Noida
Printed at: Niyogi Offset Pvt. Ltd., New Delhi, India

Introduction

Rabindranath got the inspiration to compose the poetic play *Malini* from the story 'Malinyavastu' of the Buddhist literary compendium *Mahavastu-Avadana*. He did not have access to the original; but among the books that he always carried with him during his zamindari days in North Bengal and Odisha was Rajendralal Mitra's seminal work, *The Sanskrit Buddhist Literature of Nepal*. He found the story of Malini in this anthology and basing on it wrote the verse-play in 1896, although it was first published as an independent book by Indian Publishing House some sixteen years later in 1912.

Tagore first translated *Malini* into English in the same year (1912), keeping it close to the original and retaining all the four scenes. He essayed a new translation in 1916 on the way to Japan. In this translation, four scenes of the original were condensed into two scenes, lengthy dialogues were substantially pruned, and a minor character, Prince, who did not exist in the original, was introduced in the translation. When McMillan, New York, brought out the volume *Sacrifice and Other Plays* in 1917, it is this translation which was included in the volume along with *Sannyasi , Sacrifice,* and *The King and the Queen.* Edward Thompson has commented on this translation in his book, *Rabindranath Tagore*: *His life and Work:* "It is translated fairly faithfully except that its long beautiful speeches are cut down and the first scene's opening in which Malini receives the sage Kasyapa's last instructions, is omitted."

It is interesting to learn from Tagore's preface to the Bengali original of *Malini* that Robert Trevelyn (1872-1957) found some resemblance between the play and the Greek plays. As Tagore writes, "I had a comment from Trevelyn, the poet and Greek scholar, that he noticed a resemblance between my play and the Greek drama. I could not exactly understand what he meant; though I have read a few in translation, but Greek drama is outside my experience. It is Shakespearean drama which have always been our model.'

In *Malini*, as in *Sannyasi* (Prakritir-Pratishodh) and *Sacrifice* (Visarjan) Tagore dramatized the concept that the religion of man is much higher than the religion of rituals and scriptures. Supriyo and Kshemankar are two opposite characters in the play. Supriyo believes that fair play and justice are the religion of the heart and is ready to uphold it at any cost. He does not much care for the religion based on narrow principles of caste and rituals. He is calm and composed and can be misunderstood as weak, even cowardly. He is like Binoy of *Gora*, Nikhilesh of *Ghare Baire* or Jaisingh of *Visarjan*. Kshemankar is fierce, strong, proud and dazzling in personality. Unwavering, like Raghupati of *Visarjan*, he is totally committed to the tradition of religion he has received based on Brahminism and rituals. Although Rabindranath does not himself believe in ritualistic religion and his authorial sympathy lies with Supriyo, he has not depicted Kshemankar as mean or small in any way. On the contrary, he has invested Kshemankar's character with heroic grandeur.

Malini is torn between the two heroes ------ a bond of love for Supriyo and an irrestible attraction for Kshemankar. Having recently accepted Buddhism as her faith, she suffers from a conflict between two opposing impulses—one of the ideal of universal compassion preached by Gautam Buddha and the other of love and friendship of the flesh and blood kind. When Kshemankar is imprisoned by the king on the charge of treason at the instance of Supriyo, the drama reaches its climax. After an exchange of fiery dialogues, Kshemankar hits Supriyo with his shackles and kills him on the spot. A distraught Malini still pleads with the king, her father, for showering mercy on Kshemankar. Edward Thompson finds Malini's action unconvincing, but Krishna Kripalani in his *Rabindranath Tagore: A Biography* makes the most telling analysis: "Malini, the King's daughter in the play, is his (Tagore's) first major Buddhist heroine........And yet the most powerful and convincing character in the play is not this lovely and saintly but somewhat shadowy woman in whose proud personality is symbolized the strength and obstinacy of his religion. The conflict is not only between obedience to 'moth-eaten scriptures' and religion of one's choice but between the poetry of pity and the prose of social necessity. 'Pity is beautiful like the yonder moon that casts its spell in the sky, but is that the only enduring reality? Tomorrow the day will break and the hungry multitude will draw the sea of existence with their thousand nets and their clamour will fill the sky. Then this very moon will seem a pale shadow.' But even a deeper conflict is that of personal loyalties. Should one, if faced with a relentless choice, betray one's conscience or one's religion, one's country or one's faith, the pledge of friendship or that of love? There is no answer to these questions and the tragedy of heroic folly must take its course. All that Malini can do is to forgive and ask others to forgive."

—*Nirmal Kanti Bhattacharjee*

ACT I

The Balcony of the Palace facing the street.

Malini. The moment has come for me, and my life, like the dew drop upon a lotus leaf, is trembling upon the heart of this great time. I shut my eyes and seem to hear the tumult of the sky, and there is an anguish in my heart, I know not for what.

***Enters* Queen.**

Queen. My child, what is this? Why do you forget to put on dresses that befit your beauty and youth? Where are your ornaments? My beautiful dawn, how can you absent the touch of gold from your limbs?

Malini.   Mother, there are some who are born poor, even in a king's house. Wealth does not cling to those whose destiny it is to find riches in poverty.

Queen.   That the child whose only language was the baby cry should talk to me in such riddles! My heart quakes in fear when I listen to you. Where did you pick up your new creed, which goes against all our holy books? My child, they say that the Buddhist monks, from whom you take your lessons, practice black arts; that they cast their spells upon men's minds, confounding them with lies. But I ask you, is religion a thing that one has to find by seeking? Is it not like sunlight, given to you for all days? I am a simple woman. I do not understand men's creeds and dogmas. I only know that women's true objects of worship come to their own arms, without asking, in the shape of their husbands and their children.

Enters King.

King.   My daughter, storm clouds are gathering over the King's house. Go no farther along your perilous path. Pause, if only for a short time.

Queen.   What dark words are these?

King.   My foolish child, if you must bring your new creed into this land of the old, let it not come like a sudden flood threatening those who dwell on the bank. Keep your faith to your own self. Rake not up public hatred and mockery against it.

Queen.   Do not chide my girl, and teach her the crookedness of your diplomacy. If my child should choose her own teachers and pursue her own path, I do not know who can blame her.

King.   Queen, my people are agitated, they clamour for my daughter's banishment.

Queen.   Banishment? Of your own daughter?

King. The Brahmins, frightened at her heresy, have combined, and—

Queen. Heresy indeed. Are all truths confined only in their musty, old books? Let them fling away their worm-eaten creeds, and come and take their lessons from this child. I tell you, King, she is not a common girl,—she is a pure flame of fire. Some divine spirit has taken birth in her. Do not despise her, lest some day you strike your forehead, and weep, and find her no more.

Malini. Father, grant to your people their request. The great moment has come. Banish me.

King. Why, child? What want do you feel in your father's house?

Malini. Listen to me, father. Those, who cry for my banishment, cry for me. Mother, I have no words in which to tell you what I have in my mind. Leave me without regret, like the tree that sheds its flowers unheeding. Let me go out to all men,—for the world has claimed me from the King's hands.

King. Child, I do not understand you.

Malini. Father, you are a King. Be strong and fulfil your mission.

Queen. Child, is there no place for you here, where you were born? Is the burden of the world waiting for your little shoulders?

Malini. I dream, while I am awake, that the wind is wild, and the water is troubled; the night is dark, and the boat is moored in the haven. Where is the captain, who shall take the wanderers home? I feel I know the path, and the boat will thrill with life at my touch, and speed on.

Queen. Do you hear, King? Whose words are these? Do they come from this little girl? Is she your daughter, and have I borne her?

King.   Yes, even as the night bears the dawn,—
             the dawn that is not of the night, but of
             all the world.

Queen.   King, have you nothing to keep her
             bound to your house,— this image of
             light?—My darling, your hair has come
             loose on your shoulders. Let me bind
             it up.—Do they talk of banishment,
             King? If this be a part of their creed,
             then let come the new religion, and
             let those Brahmins be taught afresh
             what is truth.

King.   Queen, let us take away our child from
             this balcony. Do you see the crowd
             gathering in the street?
                                    [*They all go out.*]

**Enter a crowd of Brahmins, in the street,
before the palace balcony. They shout.**

Brahmins.   Banishment of the King's daughter!

Kemankar.   Friends, keep your resolution firm. The
             woman, as an enemy, is to be dreaded
             more than all others. For reason is futile

against her and forces are ashamed;
man's power gladly surrenders
itself to her powerlessness, and she
takes her shelter in the strongholds of
our own hearts.

First Brahmin. We must have audience with our King,
to tell him that a snake has raised its
poisonous hood from his own nest,
and is aiming at the heart of our
sacred religion.

Supriya.   Religion? I am stupid. I do not
understand you. Tell me, sir, is it your
religion that claims the banishment of
an innocent girl?

First Brahmin. You are a marplot, Supriya, you are
ever a hindrance to all our enterprises.

Second Brahmin. We have united in defence of our faith,
and you come like a subtle rift in the
wall, like a thin smile on the compressed
lips of contempt.

Supriya.   You think that, by the force of numbers,
you will determine truth, and drown
reason by your united shouts?

First Brahmin. This is rank insolence, Supriya.

Supriya. The insolence is not mine but theirs who shape their scripture to fit their own narrow hearts.

Second Brahmin. Drive him out. He is none of us.

First Brahmin. We have all agreed upon the banishment of the Princess.—He who thinks differently, let him leave this assembly.

Supriya. Brahmins, it was a mistake on your part to elect me as one of your league. I am neither your shadow, nor an echo of your texts. I never admit that truth sides with the shrillest voice and I am ashamed to own as mine a creed that depends on force for its existence. [*To Kemankar*] Dear friend, let me go.

Kemankar. No, I will not. I know you are firm in your action, only doubting when you debate. Keep silence, my friend; for the time is evil.

Supriya. Of all things the blind certitude of stupidity is the hardest to bear. To think of saving your religion by banishing a girl from her home! But let me know what is her offence. Does she not maintain that truth and love are the body and soul of religion? If so, is that not the essence of all creeds?

Kemankar. Religion is one in its essence, but different in its forms. The water is one, yet by its different banks it is bounded and preserved for different peoples. What if you have a well-spring of your own in your heart, spurn not your neighbours who must go for their draught of water to their ancestral pond with the green of its gradual slopes mellowed by ages and its ancient trees bearing eternal fruit.

Supriya. I shall follow you, my friend, as I have ever done in my life, and not argue.

Enters Third Brahmin.

Third Brahmin. I have good news. Our words have

prevailed, and the King's army is about to take our side openly.

Second Brahmin. The army?—I do not quite like it.

First Brahmin. Nor do I. It smells of rebellion.

Second Brahmin. Kemankar, I am not for such extreme measures.

First Brahmin. Our faith will give us victory, not our arms. Let us make penance, and recite sacred verses. Let us call on the names of our guardian gods.

Second Brahmin. Come, Goddess, whose wrath is the sole weapon of thy worshippers, deign to take form and crush even to dust the blind pride of unbelievers. Prove to us the strength of our faith, and lead us to victory.

All. We invoke thee, Mother, descend from thy heavenly heights and do thy work among mortals.

Enters **Malini.**

Malini. I have come.

[*They all bow to her, except Kemankar and Supriya, who stand aloof and watch.*]

Second Brahmin. Goddess.—Thou hast come at last, as a daughter of man, withdrawing all thy terrible power into the tender beauty of a girl. Whence hast thou come, Mother? What is thy wish?

Malini. I have come down to my exile at your call.

Second Brahmin. To exile from heaven, because thy children of earth have called thee?

First Brahmin. Forgive us, Mother. Utter ruin threatens this world and it cries aloud for thy help.

Malini. I will never desert you. I always knew that your doors were open for me. The cry went from you for my banishment and I woke up, amidst the wealth and pleasure of the King's house.

Kemankar. The Princess.

All. The King's daughter.

Malini. I am exiled from my home, so that I may make your home my own. Yet tell me truly, have you need of me? When I lived in seclusion, a lonely girl, did you call to me from the outer world? Was it no dream of mine?

First Brahmin. Mother, you have come, and taken your seat in the heart of our hearts.

Malini. I was born in a King's house, never once looking out from my window. I had heard that it was a sorrowing world,— the world out of my reach. But I did not know where it felt its pain. Teach me to find this out.

First Brahmin. Your sweet voice brings tears to our eyes.

Malini. The moon has just come out of those clouds. Great peace is in the sky. It seems to gather all the world in its arms, under the fold of one vast moonlight. There goes the road, losing itself among the solemn trees with their still shadows. There are the houses, and there the temple; the river bank in the distance looks dim and desolate. I seem to have come down, like a sudden shower from a cloud of dreams, into this world of men, by the roadside.

First Brahmin. You are the divine soul of this world.

Second Brahmin. Why did not our tongues burst in pain, when they shouted for your banishment?

First Brahmin. Come, Brahmins, let us restore our Mother to her home. [*They shout.*] Victory to the Mother of the world! Victory to the Mother in the heart of the Man's daughter!
[*Malini goes, surrounded by them.*]

Kemankar. Let the illusion vanish. Where are you going, Supriya, like one walking in his sleep?

Supriya.   Leave hold of me, let me go.

Kemankar.   Control yourself. Will you, too, fly
                   into the fire with the rest of the blinded
                   swarm?

Supriya.   Was it a dream, Kemankar?

Kemankar.   It was nothing but a dream. Open your
                   eyes, and wake up.

Supriya.   Your hope of heaven is false, Kemankar.
                   Vainly have I wandered in the wilderness
                   of doctrines,—I never found peace.
                   The God, who belongs to the multitude,
                   and the God of the books are not my
                   own God. These never answered my
                   questions and never consoled me. But,
                   at last, I have found the divine breathing
                   and alive in the living world of men.

Kemankar.   Alas, my friend, it is a fearful moment
                   when a man's heart deceives him. Then
                   blind desire becomes his gospel and
                   fancy usurps the dread throne of his
                   gods. Is yonder moon, lying asleep

among soft fleecy clouds, the true emblem of ever-lasting reality? The naked day will come to-morrow, and the hungry crowd begin again to drag the sea of existence with their thousand nets. And then this moon-light night will hardly be remembered, but as a thin film of unreality made of sleep and shadows and delusions. The magic web, woven of the elusive charms of a woman, is like that,—and can it take the place of highest truth? Can any creed, born of your fancy, satisfy the gaping thirst of the midday, when it is wide awake in its burning heat?

Supriya. Alas, I know not.

Kemankar. Then shake yourself up from your dreams, and look before you. The ancient house is on fire, whose nurslings are the ages. The spirits of our forefathers are hovering over the impending ruins, like crying birds over their perishing nests. Is this the time for vacillation, when the night is dark, the enemies knocking at the gate, the citizens asleep, and men drunken with delusions laying their hands upon their brothers' throats?

Supriya. I will stand by you.

Kemankar. I must go away from here.

Supriya. Where? And for what?

Kemankar. To foreign lands. I shall bring soldiers from outside. For this conflagration cries for blood, to be quenched.

Supriya. But our own soldiers are ready.

Kemankar. Vain is all hope of help from them. They, like moths, are already leaping into the fire. Do you not hear how they are shouting like fools? The whole town has gone mad, and is lighting her festival lamps at the funeral pyre of her own sacred faith.

Supriya. If you must go, take me with you.

Kemankar.	No. You remain here, to watch and keep me informed But, friend, let your heart be not drawn away from me by the novelty of the falsehood.
Supriya.	Falsehood is new, but our friendship is old. We have ever been together from our childhood. This is our first separation.
Kemankar.	May it prove our last! In evil times the strongest bonds give way. Brothers strike brothers and friends turn against friends. I go out in to the dark, and in the darkness of night I shall come back to the gate. Shall I find my friend watching for me, with the lamp lighted? I take away that hope with me.

[*They go.*]

Enter King, *with the* Prince, *in the balcony.*

King.	I fear I must decide to banish my daughter.
Prince.	Yes, Sire, delay will be dangerous.
King.	Gently, my son, gently. Never doubt

that I will do my duty. Be sure I will
banish her.

[*Prince goes.*]

Enters Queen.

Queen.   Tell me, King, where is she? Have you
hidden her, even from me?

King.   Whom?

Queen.   My Malini.

King.   What? Is she not in her room?

Queen.   No, I cannot find her. Go with your
soldiers and search for her through all
the town, from house to house. The
citizens have stolen her. Banish them
all. Empty the whole town, till they
return her.

King.   I will bring her back,—even if my
Kingdom goes to ruin.

**The Brahmins and soldiers bring Malini,
*with torches lighted.***

Queen.   My darling, my cruel child. I never keep my eyes off you,— how could you evade me, and go out?

Second Brahmin.   Do not be angry with her, Queen. She came to our home to give us her blessings.

First Brahmin. Is she only yours? And does she not belong to us as well?

Second Brahmin.   Our little mother, do not forget us. You are our star, to lead us across the pathless sea of life.

Malini.   My door has been opened for you. These walls will never-more separate us.

Brahmins. Blessed are we, and the land where we were born.

                              [*They go.*]

Malini.   Mother, I have brought the outer world into your house. I seem to have lost the bounds of my body. I am one with the life of this world.

Queen.	Yes, child. Now you shall never need to go out. Bring in the world to you, and to your mother. It is close upon the second watch of the night. Sit here. Calm yourself. This flaming life in you is burning out all sleep from your eyes.
Malini [*embracing her mother*].	Mother, I am tired. My body is trembling. So vast is this world.— Mother dear, sing me to sleep. Tears come to my eyes, and a sadness descends upon my heart.

ACT II

The Palace Garden

Malini.   What can I say to you? I do not know how to argue. I have not read your books.

Supriya.   I am learned only among the fools of learning. I have left all arguments and books behind me. Lead me, princess, and I shall follow you, as the shadow follows the lamp.

Malini.   But, Brahmin, when you question me, I lose all my power and do not know how to answer you. It is a wonder to me to see that even you, who know everything, come to me with your questions.

Supriya.   Not for knowledge I come to you. Let me forget all that I have ever known. Roads there are, without number, but the light is missing.

Malini.   Alas, sir, the more you ask me, the more I feel my poverty. Where is that voice in me, which came down from heaven, like an unseen flash of lightning, into my heart? Why did you not come that day, but keep away in doubt? Now that I have met the world face to face my heart has grown timid, and I do not know how to hold the helm of the great ship that I must guide. I feel I am alone, and the world is large, and ways are many, and the light from the sky comes of a sudden to vanish the next moment. You who are wise and learned, will you help me?

Supriya.   I shall deem myself fortunate, if you ask my help.

Malini.   There are times when despair comes to choke all the life-currents; when suddenly, amidst crowds of men,

my eyes turn upon myself and I am
frightened. Will you befriend me in
those moments of blankness, and utter
me one word of hope that will bring me
back to life.

Supriya.   I shall keep myself ready. I shall make
my heart simple and pure, and my mind
peaceful, to be able truly to serve you.

Enters Attendant.

Attendant.   The citizens have come, asking to
see you.

Malini.   Not today. Ask their pardon for me. I
must have time to fill my exhausted
mind, and have rest to get rid of
weariness. [*Attendant goes.*] Tell me
again about Kemankar, your friend. I
long to know what your life has been
and its trials.

Supriya.   Kemankar is my friend, my brother,
my master. His mind has been firm
and strong, from early days, while my
thoughts are always flickering with

doubts. Yet he has ever kept me close
to his heart, as the moon does its dark
spots; But, however strong a ship may
be, if it harbours a small hole in its
bottom, it must sink.—That I would
make you sink, Kemankar, was in the
law of nature.

Malini.   You made him sink?

Supriya.   Yes, I did. The day when the rebellion
slunk away in shame before the light
in your face and the music in the air
touched you, Kemankar alone was
unmoved. He left me behind him, and
said that he must go to the foreign land
to bring soldiers, and uproot the new
creed from the sacred soil of Kashi.—
You know what followed. You made me
live again in a new land of birth. 'Love
for all life' was a mere word, waiting
from the old time to be made real,—and
I saw that truth in you in flesh. My heart
cried for my friend, but he was away,
out of my reach; then came his letter,
in which he wrote that he was coming
with a foreign army at his back, to wash

away the new faith in blood, and to
punish you with death.—I could wait no
longer. I showed the letter to the King.

Malini.

Why did you forget yourself, Supriya?
Why did fear overcome you? Have I
not room enough in my house for him
and his soldiers?

***Enters* King.**

King.

Come to my arms, Supriya, I went at
a fit time to surprise Kemankar and
to capture him. An hour later, and a
thunderbolt would have burst upon my
house in my sleep. You are my friend,
Supriya, come—

Supriya.

God forgive me.

King.

Do you not know, that a King's love is
not unsubstantial? I give you leave to
ask for any reward that comes to your
mind. Tell me, what do you want?

Supriya.

Nothing, Sire, nothing. I shall live,
begging from door to door.

King.   Only ask me, and you shall have provinces worthy to tempt a king.

Supriya.   They do not tempt me.

King.   I understand you. I know towards what moon you raise your hands. Mad youth, be brave to ask even that which seems so impossible. Why are you silent? Do you remember the day when you prayed for my Malini's banishment? Will you repeat that prayer to me, to lead my daughter to exile from her father's house?—My daughter, do you know that you owe your life to this noble youth? And is it hard for you to payoff that debt with your—?

Supriya.   For pity's sake, Sire, no more of this. Worshippers there are many who by life-long devotion have gained the highest fulfillment of their desire. Could I be counted one of them I should be happy. But to accept it from the King's hands as the reward of treachery? Lady mine, you have the plenitude and peace of your greatness; you know not the secret cravings of a poverty-stricken soul. I dare not ask from you an atom more than that pity of love which you have for every creature in the world.

Malini.   Father, what is your punishment for the captive?

King.   He shall die.

Malini.   On my knees I beg from you his pardon.

King.   But he is a rebel, my child.

Supriya.   Do you judge him, King? He also judged you, when he came to punish you, not to rob your kingdom.

Malini.   Spare him his life, father. Then only will you have the right to bestow on him your friendship, who has saved you from a great peril.

King.   What   do   you   say,   Supriya?

Shall I restore a friend to his
friend's arms?

Supriya.   That will be king-like in its grace.

King.   It will come in its time, and you will
find back your friend. But a King's
generosity must not stop there. I must
give you something which exceeds
your hope,—yet not as a mere reward.
You have won my heart, and my heart
is ready to offer you its best treasure.—
My child, where was this shyness in
you before now? Your dawn had no
tint of rose,—its light was white and
dazzling. But to-day a tearful mist of
tenderness sweetly tempers it for mortal
eyes. [*To Supriya*] Leave my feet, rise
up and come to my heart. Happiness
is pressing it like pain. Leave me now
for a while. I want to be alone with my
Malini. [*Supriya goes.*] I feel I have
found back my child once again,—
not the bright star of the sky, but the
sweet flower that blossoms on earthly
soil. She is my daughter, the darling of
my heart.

Enters Attendant.

Attendant.   The captive, Kemankar, is at the door.

King.   Bring him in. Here comes he, with his eyes fixed, his proud head held high, a brooding shadow on his forehead, like a thunder cloud motionless in a suspended storm.

Malini.   The iron chain is shamed of itself upon those limbs. The insult to greatness is its own insult. He looks like a god defying his captivity.

Enters **Kemankar** *in chains.*

King.   What punishment do you expect from my hands?

Kemankar.   Death.

King.   But if I pardon you?

Kemankar.   Then I shall have time again to complete the work I began.

King.   You seem out of love with your life. Tell me your last wish, if you have any.

Kemankar.   I want to see my friend, Supriya, before I die.

King [*to the Attendant*].   Ask Supriya to come.

Malini.   There is a power in that face that frightens me. Father, do not let Supriya come.

King.   Your fear is baseless, child.

Supriya *enters, and walks towards* **Kemankar,** *with arms extended.*

Kemankar.   No, no, not yet. First let us have our say, and then the greeting of love.—Come closer to me. You know I am poor in words,—and my time is short. My trial is over, but not yours. Tell me, why have you done this?

Supriya.   Friend, you will not understand me. I had to keep my faith, even at the cost of my love.

Kemankar.   I understand you, Supriya. I have seen
                that girl's face, glowing with an inner
                light, looking like a voice becoming
                visible. You offered, to the fire of those
                eyes, the faith in your' fathers' creed,
                the faith in your country's good, and
                built up a new one on the foundation of
                a treason.

Supriya.   Friend, you are right. My faith has
                come to me perfected in the form of
                that woman. Your sacred books were
                dumb to me. I have read, by the help of
                the light of those eyes, the ancient book
                of creation, and I have known that true
                faith is there, where there is man, where
                there is love. It comes from the mother
                in her devotion, and it goes back to her
                from her child. It descends in the gift
                of a giver and it appears in the heart of
                him who takes it. I accepted the bond
                of this faith which reveals the infinite
                in man, when I set my eyes upon that
                face full of light and love and peace of
                hidden wisdom.

Kemankar.   I also once set my eyes on that face, and

for a moment dreamt that religion had come at last, in the form of a woman, to lead man's heart to heaven. For a moment, music broke out from the very ribs of my breast and all my life's hopes blossomed in their fullness. Yet did not I break through these meshes of illusion to wander in foreign lands? Did not I suffer humiliation from unworthy hands in patience, and bear the pain of separation from you, who have been my friend from my infancy? And what have you been doing meanwhile? You sat in the shade of the King's garden, and spent your sweet leisure in idly weaving a lie to condone your infatuation and calling it a religion.

Supriya.   My friend, is not this world wide, enough to hold men whose natures are widely different? Those countless stars of the sky, do they fight for the mastery of the One? Cannot faiths hold their separate lights in peace for the separate worlds of minds that need them?

Kemankar.   Words, mere words. To let falsehood

and truth live side by side in amity, the infinite world is not wide enough. That the corn ripening for the food of man should make room for thorny weeds, love is not so hatefully all-loving. That one should be allowed to sap the sure ground of friendship with betrayal of trust, could tolerance be so treacherously wide as that? That one should die like a thief to defend his faith and the other live in honour and wealth who betrayed it—no, no, the world is not so stony-hearted as to bear without pain such hideous contradictions in its bosom.

Supriya
[*to Malini*].

All these hurts and insults I accept in your name, my lady, Kemankar, you are paying your life for your faith,—I am paying more. It is your love, dearer than my life.

Kemankar.

No more of this prating. All truths must be tested in death's court. My friend, do you remember our student days when we used to wrangle the whole night through, to come at last to our teacher, in the morning, to know in a moment which of us was right? Let that morning break now. Let us go there to that land of the final, and stand before death with all our questions, where the changing mist of doubts will vanish at a breath, and the mountain peaks of eternal truth will appear, and we two fools will look at each other and laugh.—Dear friend, bring before death that which you deem your best and immortal.

Supriya.   Friend, let it be as you wish.

Kemankar.   Then come to my heart. You had wandered far from your comrade, in the infinite distance,—now, dear friend, come eternally close to me, and accept from one, who loves you, the gift of death. [*Strikes Supriya with his chains, and Supriya falls.*]

Kemankar.   [*embracing the dead body of Supriya*]. Now call your executioner.

King   Where is my sword?
[*rising up*].

Malini.   Father, forgive Kemankar!

Other Classics in the Tagore Series

- The King of the Dark Chamber

- Fire Flies

- Fruit Gathering

- Gitanjali

- Nationalism

- Red Oleanders

- Religion of man

- Sacrifice

- The Crescent Moon

- The Crown

- The Fugitive